# The Little Book of Zen Meditation

Scott Shaw

Buddha Rose Publications

The Little Book of Zen Meditation
Copyright © 2009 by Scott Shaw
www.scottshaw.com
All Rights Reserved

No part of this book may be reproduced in any manner without the expressed written permission of the author or the publishing company.

ISBN: 1877792500
ISBN-13: 9781877792502

First Edition 2009

Library of Congress Control Number:
2009941807

Cover Photograph © 1985 Scott Shaw
Buddha: Bangkok, Thailand

Disclaimer: The author and the publishers of this book are in no way responsible, in any manner whatsoever, for any injury that may result from practicing the techniques presented in this book. Since the practices discussed in this book may be too strenuous for some readers, it is highly suggested that you consult your physician before you undertake any physical activities.

10 9 8 7 6 5 4 3 2 1
Printed in the United States of America

# The Little Book
*of Zen Meditation*

# Table of Contents

## PART I
**Zen Buddhism:**
   **The Meditative Practices**  7

1 Zazen  9
2 The Zen Koan  21
3 Kinhin: Walking Meditation  25
4 Zen Buddhism and the Arts  33

## PART II
**The Metaphysical Aspects
   of Zen Buddhism**  49

5 The Mind of No Mind  51

## PART III
**Nirvana**  61

6 Nirvana: The Formalities  63
7 The Three Buddha  67
8 Understanding Enlightenment  71

About the Author  79
Scott Shaw: *Books-In-Print*  81

# PART I
## Zen Buddhism:
### The Meditative Practices

At the heart of Zen Buddhism is the practice of meditation. Meditation is a formalized technique where the mind is calmed and the practitioner is allowed to come into contact with the *Buddha-mind*. It is understood that only through a perfectly centered mind is an individual ever able to merge *individual-self* with the *universal-self* and reach the ultimate state of human existence, enlightenment.

Zen Buddhism is not full of a plethora of meditative techniques as is the case with some of the other schools of eastern mysticism. Though there are a few variations to the primary Zen Buddhist meditative practice of *Zazen*, they are all based in a single focal point; focusing the mind to the degree where it may encounter *Nirvana*. *Nirvana* is the state where the *individual-mind* meets the *universal-mind* and one embraces enlightenment.

# Chapter 1
## Zazen

*Zazen* is the practice of formal meditation used in Zen Buddhism. In Japanese, *"Za"* means to be seated. *"Zazen,"* therefore, means, *"To be seated in Zen."*

The practice of meditation has been handed down for centuries as a method for one to come into contact with divine understanding. *Zazen* is the Zen Buddhist application of this ancient practice.

### The Seat

In Zen Buddhism, meditation is referred to as, *"Shikantaza."* Literally translated, this Japanese word means, *"Just Sitting."* With this as a definition, in English, *Zazen* is commonly referred to as, *"Sitting."*

It is understood that *your-seat*, meaning the way you are seated, is one of the most essential elements in proper meditation. For this reason, the Zen Buddhism practitioner very consciously sits down and steadies himself in his seated posture before he ever begins to meditate.

The Sanskrit word, *"Asana,"* is often used to describe the seated posture for meditation. Translated from the Sanskrit, *"Asana,"* means, *"Seat or Throne."*

The classic posture for seated meditation is, *"Padma Asana,"* or, *"The Lotus Pose."* This is where the practitioner sits cross-legged on the ground.

There are three variations of this posture. The first and most basic is, *"Sukh Asana."* This is where the legs are naturally crossed and the feet touch the ground underneath the thighs. The second is, *"Arddha Padma Asana,"* or *"Half Lotus."* In Japanese, this posture is referred to as, *"Hankafuza."* Hankafuza is where the top of one foot is brought up and placed on the thigh of the opposite leg.

The third meditative posture is, *"Padma Asana,"* or, *"Full Lotus."* In Japanese this posture is known as, *"Kekkafuza."* Kekkafuza is where the right foot is placed on the left thigh and the left foot is placed upon the right thigh.

For centuries it has been taught that *Kekkafuza* is the most beneficial posture to assume while meditating. It is stated throughout ancient texts that this pose is the most foundationally firm, as it locks the body tightly into place and, thereby, allows the mind to focus solely upon meditation.

Though *Kekkafuza* is understood to be the ideal posture for meditation, it is uncomfortable for many individuals to sit in this position for extended periods of time. Ultimately, *Zazen* is about the practice of meditation. So, if you cannot comfortably sit in this pose for long periods of time, then you should sit in whatever position you can comfortably maintain, including sitting in a firm chair, as you perform *Zazen*.

Many times, the Zen Buddhist practitioner, when seated in any of the meditative lotus postures, will sit upon a small mat, known in Japanese as, *"Zabuton."* Upon the mat sits a small pillow, *"Zafu."* The practitioner then sits upon these two objects as he meditates.

Some schools of Buddhism believe that this creates too soft of a seat for a practitioner to truly meditate. Others believe that by adding a bit of comfort it will actually aid in the meditative process. Ultimately, it is you who must decide what works best for your body and your mind as you practice *Zazen*.

## Seiza

The Zen Buddhist also uses another position for seated meditation -- the kneeling pose. This posture is known in Japanese as, *"Seiza."* The kneeling posture is achieved by placing both of your knees on the floor, separated at the distance of your shoulders. The tops of your feet are encountering the ground and your right big toe is placed atop your left big toe. In this position, your spine should be kept erect, as with the lotus posture. Once you are seated in this position, you place your hands face down, naturally atop each of your legs.

## Firm Seat

To correctly perform *Zazen* your body must be kept in a firm positioning. Your spine must be kept erect, so your internal energy will continue to flow in a constantly ascending pattern.

The Japanese Buddhist term, *"Fudo no Shisei,"* means *"Immovable Posture."* This is essential to *Zazen*. So, whatever meditative posture you decide to take, you must be able to firmly formalize your body into that posture and remain unmovable throughout your meditation. With a firm seat, your mind can concentrate upon your meditation and not be distracted by physical movement or discomfort.

## The Hands in Zazen

Once you have settled into your seated posture, it is important that you consciously straighten your spine. From this, your back muscles do not become strained and energy is allowed to flow unimpeded up and down your spine.

With you body in a firm posture, you will then place your hands in what is known in Japanese as, *"Hokkaijo in,"* This means, *"Hands in perfect balance with the universe."*

The Japanese word, *"In"* is a translation of the Sanskrit word, *"Mudra,"* which means to seal. To form an *In*, you place your hands in a very precise formation.

The ideal *Hokkaijo In* for *Zazen* occurs when you lay your right hand in your lap with your palm open, facing upward. You place your left hand loosely on top of it. You then allow the tips of your thumb to lightly touch.

### Hara

The *Hara* is the body's natural center of gravity. This bodily location exists approximately four inches below the navel. In addition, *Hara* is the bodily location where *Ki, "Universal Energy,"* congregates and is dispersed. For this reason, the *Hara* is one of the most sacred locations on the human body.

*Hara* is located approximately four inches below the navel. From this central location it expands approximately two inches in each direction. In Buddhist scriptures *Hara* is referred to as, *"Tanden." Tanden* means, *"The burning place of energy."*

The Zen Buddhist practitioner of meditation understands that it is essential to become highly focused upon this revered location in order to not only readily tap into and utilize *Ki* energy but to additionally remain consciously balanced in all of life's activities, particularly meditation, as well. For this reason, as one prepares for *Zazen* they initially focus their attention upon this location and consciously find a balance in their seat before they begin the formal practice of meditation.

## Open Your Eyes

It is commonly understood that the various techniques of meditation are to be performed with the eyes closed. For obvious reasons, with your eyes closed, you are less prone to be distracted by external images. The Buddhist meditation of *Zazen,* however, is performed with your eyes slightly open -- loosely gazing at a visually stagnant location approximately three feet in front of you upon the floor. Some schools of *Zazen* place an actual dot on the floor in front of the practitioner in order to give them a physical placement of focus.

The reason the eyes are left partially open in *Zazen* is threefold. First of all, by leaving your eyes partially open, you keep yourself associated with the fact that you possess a physical body. In Zen, you never negate this fact, as do various schools of Yoga. Instead, you embrace the fact that your soul is located in a physical being and that this body is your pathway to the *Buddha-mind.* Secondarily, by holding your eyes slightly open you do not allow yourself to enter into a dream-like state of sleep, where your mind can drift to fantasies. Finally, it is understood that the process of Zen meditation leads one down the path of an acutely focused mind. By locking your vision onto a single spot on the floor, you train your thinking-mind to become acutely controlled. From this, you possess much more authority over the experiences of your physical body and emotional mentality than does the average person. You can, in fact, as the depth of your meditation increases, control such things as your physical and mental reaction to injury, pain, and emotionally debilitating life situations.

## Wall Staring

In certain schools of Zen Buddhism the technique of, *"Tai Ch'ng Pi Kwan"* or *"Wall Staring"* is used to achieve the objective of leaving your eyes partially opened while limiting the amount of possible external visual stimuli. In this case, the practitioner locates a spot on the wall slightly below eye level and locks his vision onto it and uses it as his point of focus.

## Beginning Zazen

To begin *Zazen,* sit upon the floor and allow yourself to become integrated with your seated posture for a few moments. Once you feel stationary, firm, and comfortable, begin to observe your breath. Do not attempt to control it, simply allow it to enter and exit your body, via your nose, naturally. Once your mind has grown accustomed to this process, begin to attach the number, *"One,"* to each in-breath and the number, *"Two,"* to each out-breath. Mentally repeat, *"One, Two." "One, Two."*

It is understood that your mind will tend to wander when you first begin to practice *Zazen*. Mentally counting will help to bring your concentration back to the life giving process of breathing.

## Stop Thinking

The purpose of *Zazen* is to still your mind. Therefore, you do not want to think, visualize, or fantasize when you are practicing *Zazen*.

When you first begin the practice, thoughts will naturally form in your mind. This is because of the fact, for most of your life you have allowed your thoughts to rapidly move from one thought onto the next. Thus, your mind is trained to interact with life in this fashion.

If you find yourself thinking during *Zazen,* do not be upset with yourself, simply refocus your consciousness on your *One, Two* counting and again embrace your thoughtless *Buddha-mind.*

### How Long?

Most schools of Zen have their students perform *Zazen* in group sessions for forty-five to fifty minutes. This is understood to be the ideal amount of time for meditation as it provides the practitioner with enough time to truly focus his mind.

For the student who is in the early stages of *Zazen* practice, however, sitting for this amount of time is not required. This is especially the case, if the new practitioner is performing this technique alone.

The physical state of being alone and solitary is good for *Zazen.* This is due to the fact that while alone, there is less of a chance for distractions. While *Sitting* alone, however, it is understood that the mind of the novice meditator will tend to race from thought-to-thought more readily than if he was in a group. From this, the student may become disillusioned with his inability to meditate.

For this reason, when practicing *Zazen* alone, in the early stages, it can be practiced for approximately twenty minutes, twice a day -- generally in the morning and in the evening. By performing *Zazen* for this amount of time, one can learn how to calm the mind and embrace the conscious emptiness of Zen without feeling forced to sit for an uncomfortable amount of time.

### Hishiryo

The practice of *Zazen* allows the mind to become silent. Thinking is defined in Japanese as, *"Shiryo."* Not thinking is *"Fushiro." Zazen,* however, leads the practitioner to the more advanced state of consciousness known as, *"Hishiryo," "Without thinking."*

*Hishiryo* is thought without thought. From this state, *pure-consciousness* is encountered. When the individual embraces *pure-consciousness,* the mind is not held captive by desire. Without desire the individual mind realizes its own *Buddha-nature*. From this, oneness with all elements of the universe is embraced.

When the mind is allowed to be silent, *perfect action* is accomplished. This is because of the fact that no action is attempted. *Action within no action is the paradoxical essence of Zen.*

The action of no action is the basis of enlightenment. Thus, *Zazen* is paramount to the development of the individual in Zen Buddhism.

## Chapter 2
## The Zen Koan

The Rinzai School of Zen Buddhism, founded by Myoan Eisai, teaches that enlightenment may come in a burst of instantaneous cosmic understanding. This school of thought details that though one must meditate to realize the ultimate state of human existence; the actual experiences come in a flash of *pure-consciousness*. For this reason, the Rinzai School emphasizes the use of the *Zen Koan* as one of the primary pathways to enlightenment.

The *Zen Koan* is a statement generally presented in the form of a question. The *Koan* is designed to cause the Zen practitioner to alter his course of normal thinking and be forced into a new reality, where the enlightened mind may be encountered.

The most common example of a *Zen Koan* is, *"What is the sound of one hand clapping?"*

The early foundations of the *Koan* can be traced back to the Chinese Tang Dynasty (618-907 CE). In Chinese, the term *Koan* is, *"Gong-an."* This term originally detailed an established principal or accepted law. As the term evolved and became embraced by Zen Buddhist philosophy, this *"Established principal,"* came to represent the deeper understanding of cosmic reality.

## The Practice

A teacher, or, *"Roshi,"* in Japanese, presents a *Koan* to the student in a private session known in Japanese as, *"Dokusan."* The student then presents an answer to his teacher.

There is no one correct answer for a *Koan*. The answer given simply reflects the student's understanding of life, Zen, and enlightenment. The purest answers are understood to arise from the enlightened *inner-being* of the student. For this reason, the answer is never thought-out. It is simply expressed.

In many cases, if the *Roshi* is not satisfied with the answer, he or she will instruct the student to go back and meditate on the *Koan*. This meditation is not the student taking the *Koan* back with him, sitting down, and trying to figure out the best answer. Instead, it is a process where the student meditates upon the *Koan,* until the essence of the

*Koan* is embraced by the meditative non-thinking mind. At this stage, when the *Roshi* poses the *Koan* again, a new, more pure answer is revealed. Ultimately, it is understood that the Zen practitioner will embrace *Satori* by peering deeply into the meaning of the *Koan*.

## Chapter 3
## Kinhin
*Walking Meditation*

Meditation is not limited to *Sitting* in Zen Buddhism. It is understood that the practitioner must ultimately bring meditation into every element of his life if he hopes to meet enlightenment. For this reason, there are techniques of movement meditation that may be brought into the overall Zen meditative practice, even in the early stages of a student's meditative development.

The Japanese term, *"Kinhin,"* describes a walking style of meditation. *Kinhin* is often times used in the *Zendo "Meditation Hall,"* to give the meditative practitioner a break during long periods of seated meditation.

*Kinhin* begins when a bell in the *Zendo* rings twice. This occurrence is known in Japanese as, *"Kinhinsho."* At this point, the *Zazen* practitioner arises and *Kinhin* begins.

## The Practice

*Kinhin* is a very formal practice of walking meditation. It is not simply a chance to stand up and loosen the legs. When the bell rings, the Zen practitioner arises, very consciously, while placing his left hand, in the style of a fist, into his right hand -- which grasps this fist. This *Mudra* is known as, *"Shashu,"* in Japanese. The eyes are then lowered to the ground, just in front of the practitioner. The walking meditation then, very consciously, commences in a clockwise direction around the *Zendo*. The steps are very small and each one is taken with focused consciousness.

As with *Zazen,* the focus of *Kinhin* is placed upon the breath. In *Kinhin* a breath is taken in association with each step. The in-breath is very consciously taken in and a small step is made. The out-breath is exhaled, as another small step is taken.

## Moving Outward

*Kinhin* is not limited to simply walking around the *Zendo*. The conscious practitioner can elevate this meditative practice and bring it into each walk he takes.

As Zen is a pathway of consciousness, walking in *Kinhin* can truly bring spiritual understanding into new areas of the practitioner's life. In fact, there are many modern schools of Buddhism that use *Kinhin* as one of their primary practices outside of the *Zendo*.

To make *Kinhin* part of your ongoing life meditation, all you have to do is remain very conscious of your breath as you move outside and begin to take a walk. Just as in *Zazen*, this takes some practice.

Practice of *Kinhin* is necessary, due to the fact that when you are inside, in a quiet environment, with no movement to distract you, it is much easier to remain consciously focused and to catch yourself when your thoughts begin to wonder. When you are exposed to the sights and sounds of the external world, however, it is much harder to remain consciously focused.

By bringing your meditation out to the world, not only do you cause yourself to redefine your understanding of meditation but also you become a positive conduit to the material world around you.

## Focusing

To take *Kinhin* to the outside world, you will ideally perform *Zazen* for at least a few minutes and very consciously focus your consciousness. You will want to mentally define what you are about to do. Once you feel you are appropriately centered, you will then very consciously rise, just as you would in the *Zendo* and move towards the door.

Whereas in the *Zendo* you will clasp your left fist in your right hand, as you perform *Kinhin,* this is not necessary when you take *Kinhin* out to the world. In fact, it is better that you do not bring undo attention to yourself, as this has the potential to invite distractions to your walking meditation.

While practicing *Kinhin* in the *Zendo,* you walk one small step per breath. When you take your *Kinhin* out to the world, this practice may be employed, but it is not required. This depends on your particular situation and the environment you find yourself in. If you find yourself in a very tranquil environment, then all of the formalities of *Zendo Kinhin* can be employed. But, if you are simply walking the streets of the city, the formalities can be left behind. All that needs to remain is your acutely focused mind.

## Beginning the Walk

To begin your walk, you will walk at the pace you find appropriate to your situation. You will begin by finding naturalness in your step. Your pattern of walking should not be forced. Simply allow it to be natural.

As you walk, your heart rate will naturally increase, which will increase the intensity of your breathing. So, before you begin to become focused upon your breath, allow your body to find a harmony.

At the point you feel natural in your pace, and in-tune to the beating of your heart, you will then start to consciously observe your breath. Do not force it. Do not control it. As this will cause your natural breathing patterns to be altered and it could result in your becoming light-headed from lack of oxygen or hyperventilated. Simply allow yourself to breathe appropriately to the pace of your walk.

At the point you have achieved a balance of body, mind, spirit, and breath, begin to consciously observe your breath. As you walk, watch your breath enter your body, fill your being with life giving oxygen, and then exit your body. Never attempt to control it, simply focus your consciousness upon the process.

If you wish to add the counting of *One, Two* to your movement, as a means to remain meditatively focused, do so. With each in-breath, count, *"One."* With each out-breath, count, *"Two."*

As you walk, allow yourself to experience your environment, but do not allow yourself to be controlled by it. Accept that we live in the world, and there are many things going on. You are a part of the supreme essence of this universe. Thus, you never have to be controlled by this illusionary place we call life.

Just as in *Zazen,* if you feel your thoughts slipping, bring them back to the focus of your breath. If you have to stop at a crosswalk for a passing car, simply witness the movement of life, but remain focused upon your breath.

By bringing meditation into new and uncharted elements of your life, not only do you learn to take positive control over your racing mind, but you also come into a deeper harmony with your *universal-self.* From this, you learn to maintain mental control in all life experiences -- be they bad or good. You learn to remain meditative in all life situations and never be controlled by the ever changingness of this place we call life.

## Chapter 4
## Zen Buddhism
### and the Arts

Whereas many schools of meditation focus their practices solely upon the individual finding his or her pathway to enlightenment by performing formalized seated meditation, this is not the case with Zen Buddhism. From the early Chinese schools of *Ch'an* Buddhism forward, Zen has embraced the arts as a means for the practitioner to not only focus his individual meditative consciousness but also for the Zen Master to expound his understanding of *Nirvana* to the world through various, non-traditional, methods. Painting, poetry, gardening, the preparation of flowers, food, and drink, and the martial arts are all viewed as effective means of meditation in Zen Buddhism.

The arts, as an essential element of Zen Buddhism, were initially influenced by the Taoist reverence for nature. From this reverence came a close alliance of the body and mind of the spiritualist with nature. As the centuries have progressed, the practitioners of Zen strive to become very consciously aware of the ever-moving patterns of nature. From this, they became interactive with this universal movement.

### Zen Teachings in Art

From the artistic creations of Zen Buddhist Masters, the viewer is presented with his unique concept of the essence of enlightenment. Each artistic portrayal delineates the universal understanding of communion with nature and the essential essence of human life in association with the *Buddha-mind*. From the presentation of Zen based art, the masters invoke inspiration in those who view these works. From this, they guide the practitioner down the pathway of Zen.

### Zenga

Zen art is known in Japanese as, *"Zenga."* This term actually defines the painting and the calligraphy used in association with Zen Buddhism. *Zenga* uses black ink on white paper.

Whereas many styles of art, born from religion, use very exacting detail and elaborate coloration and brush strokes to create their religious works of art, this is not the case with *Zenga*. *Zenga* presents the true essence of art by the most simplistic and refined means possible.

*Zenga* is a means of focusing the mind of the painter to the degree where the *individual-self* is lost and the true essence of the *Buddha-mind* is exposed. This is accomplished by representing an image, person, or natural scene in its most elemental form.

*Zenga* is a pathway of meditation. It is a method of bringing the artist into a natural state of contact with not only the *inner-self* but with the image that is being painted. For this reason, formality is left behind, exposing the true essence of art.

### Historic Zenga

The early expression of *Zenga* first began to be witnessed during the sixth century in China. This art form began to flourish by the twelfth century in Japan. It was highly embraced as a meditative method by Zen monks of Japan's Edo period (1615 – 1868). One of the most prominent artists of this era was Hakuin Ekaku. Hakuin not only solidified *Zenga* as an essential element of Zen Buddhism but he also helped to revitalize the, then faltering, Rinzai School of Zen.

### Hakuin Ekaku

Hakuin Ekaku (1685 - 1768) is one of the elemental figures of mid-period Japanese Zen Buddhism. Hakuin was born in the village of Hara, near the base of Mount Fuji. He decided to become a Zen monk as a child. By the age of fifteen he had won the consent of his parents to embrace the monastic lifestyle. After many years of study, travel, and personal revelations, at the age of thirty-one, he returned to his first temple, the Shoin-ji Temple, where he was installed as the abbot. At the age of forty-one, Hakuin experienced the final stage of enlightenment while reading, *"The Lotus Sutra."* From that point forward, he spent the rest of his life leading other towards *Nirvana.*

Hakuin's mastery of Zen spread across the island nation of Japan. He was frequently asked to lecture at seminal Zen temples and his writings were highly published and read. Hakuin did not begin painting until he was in his sixties. Once he started painting, however, he continued the process until his death at eighty-four. As his years progressed, he turned to painting more-and-more as a means to portray his understanding of Zen. More than any other artist in Japanese history, the paintings of Hakuin have had a profound effect on the ongoing development of *Zenga*.

## Calligraphy

The simple brush strokes of *Zenga* have proven to be an ideal tool to portray a Zen Master's understanding of enlightenment. In many cases, a single word will be used in a *Zenga* painting. In other cases, a *Koan* will be presented. As a tool of meditation, the students will not only seek the deeper meaning of the word, expression, or *Koan,* presented in the painting, but will also allow their mind to acutely focus on the presentation of the painted word or words. From this, the Zen practitioner achieves a focus for his meditation and is guided towards the *Buddha-mind* by the brush strokes of the artist.

## Portraiture

One of the common subjects of *Zenga* is painting the portrait of legendary Buddhist figures such as Bodhidharma. Though no one knows what this historical figure actually looked like, throughout the centuries, interpretations of his image have filled many paintings. In these portraitures, the Zen artist attempts to tap into the essence of these historic figures and emulate their teachings by means of art.

### Art as Meditation

Most schools of traditional art train the student in methods so that they can paint the most mirror-like representation of an existing object. Even the abstract schools of art guide the students to represent their emotions or their interpretation of life in art. *Zenga* art does not follow this formula, however.

Zen understands that emotions are temporary. They are like the waves of the ocean -- they arrive and then they retreat. Zen also understands this world is temporal. What is here today will not be here tomorrow. For this reason, attempting to grasp and hold onto a place or a moment in time only holds one bound to the illusions of this material world.

Moreover, most artists create their works of art from a space of ego. *"This is my work, my style, my interpretation, my art."* Ego holds one bound to the *thinking-mind* and to the thought of, *"I."* If an individual is bound by thinking and the ego then he can never experience the essence of the *Buddha-mind.* For this reason, the *Zenga* artist strives to completely remove him or herself from the constraints of ego. He allows the art to be the art -- not a personal creation -- simply a method of focusing and aligning the *physical-mind* with the *Buddha-mind.*

Zen is about spiritual freedom and enlightenment. It is not about personal creation. The Zen artist allows the creation to happen. He does not attempt to control, define, like or dislike what ultimately occurs. Like life, he simply allows his art to exist in its own perfection.

### The Japanese Zen Tea Ceremony

As Zen Buddhism came to flourish in Japan, many aspects of Japanese culture came to embrace the simplicity and meditative mindset of Zen. This has been the case in all aspects of Japanese culture. In fact, Japanese culture cannot be separate from Zen, due to the fact that so much of the two have intermingled and come to formulate a single cohesive unit. This is the case with the Japanese Tea Ceremony.

### Cha-no-yu

The Japanese term, *"Cha-no-yu"* literally translates as, *"Hot water for tea."* This term has come to define one of the most meditative aspects of drink preparation in recorded history. In fact, the proper preparation and presentation of the Tea Ceremony is understood to take years of practice before one has mastered the subtle realms of this technique.

### The History of the Tea Ceremony

The drinking of tea is believed to have entered Japan via the hands of Chinese Buddhist monks in the ninth century. Tea soon became a widely embraced drink throughout the island nation.

During the ninth century the drinking of tea also became a Zen based formulized practice. Lu Yo (733 - 804), sometimes credited as being, *"The Sage of Tea,"* was the first to compose a text that details how one should properly plant, cultivate, harvest, prepare, and drink tea.

Lu Yo, as an abandoned child, spent his early years in a Chinese Buddhist monastery. Refusing to become a monk, as a teenager he escaped and became a traveling clown. He eventually settled down in the Zhejiang region of China, where he became a master of the growth and preparation of tea. His writings traveled to Japan where they set the foundations for the Tea Ceremony to become a highly evolved practice.

By the sixteenth century the Tea Ceremony had become a universally embraced and revered practice in Japan. This formality was helped along by the Japanese Tea Master, Sen no Rikyu (1522 - 1591). He composed a poem that can be translated as, *"Without any spiritual training, you think you are drinking tea, but actually tea drinks you."*

From this simple inspiration, the Tea Ceremony has continued to evolve throughout the centuries as both a practice based in Japanese culture and a meditative technique. The principals set forth in the Tea Ceremony are harmony, respect, purity, and tranquility.

In the Tea Ceremony, all aspects of preparation, presentation, and consummation are viewed in the purest form. As such, the Tea Ceremony is considered one of the most revered forms of meditative practice in Japanese Zen Culture.

## Zen and the Martial Arts

Certainly, Zen Buddhism has been one of the most essential elements in the development of the martial arts. This is especially the case with the Japanese martial arts -- particularly in regards to the group of warriors that have become commonly referred to as, *"The Samurai."*

The title, *"Samurai"* is a modern term. It was never used in ancient Japan to define a warrior. The word, *"Samurai"* is based in the Japanese term *"Samurau."* This term came from the Heian period of Japanese history, which existed from 794 to 1185. *"Samurau,"* means to serve. The word, *"Samurai,"* therefore, connotes one who is in service to a master.

*"Bushi,"* is the Japanese word that actually defined the formalized military warriors. *Bushi* is the name given to those individuals who were born into families from the warrior tradition, then trained in the martial arts,

and became professional soldiers. These families were known in Japanese as, *"Buke."*

The history of the *Bushi* goes back to the seventh century in Northern Japan. This formularized trend in Japanese culture occurred when families formed into clans to fight the invasive *Ainu* from modern day Sapporo, Japan. By the twelfth century, the *Bushi* were a highly defined fighting class, who were not only battling the *Honke,* those of Noble birth, for power over the island nation, but additionally those warriors who were based in Buddhist temples, known as *Sohei.*

As the Buddhist religion came to extend over Japan, powerful Buddhist temples were substantiated. The temples came to be in possession of large amounts of farmland. The temple priests would lease the land and collect large taxes on its usage. The *Sohei* were the warriors who enforced the tax laws of the temple, as well as engaged in expansionistic battles against other Buddhist Monasteries.

The Japanese word, *"Gakusho,"* is the name for the upper hierarchy scholar priests. These priests generally drew lineage from one of the three

Japanese royal families. In addition, they controlled the *Sohei* and gained the spoils of Japanese Buddhist expansionism.

In the twelfth century, the Minamoto family overthrew the other two reigning royal families: the Fujiwara and the Taira. With their defeat, Minamoto no Yoritomo (1147 - 1199), established the first military government. This government is historically referred to as *the Kamakure Shogunate.* This Shogunate led Japan into its Kamakura Period (1192 - 1333). This came to be the foundation for the historic period of Japanese history when the military class ruled the country.

### Warfare as Meditation

As time progressed and military and Zen Buddhist hold substantiated itself over Japan, the *Bushi* progressively moved into a period where the techniques of the military arts became exercises in meditation. From this came the birth of the *Ronin*.

The Japanese term, *"Ronin,"* literally translates as, *"Wave man,"* meaning these warriors moved around and had no home. The *Ronin* were wandering warriors -- not completely different from the *Sadhu,* *"Homeless monks"* of India, except in the fact that they were extensively trained in the arts of warfare.

The *Ronin* were Zen based warriors, who, in association with Zen Priests, developed the martial arts of Japan to the level where expertise in warfare was not the only goal in becoming a skilled military technician. Instead, it was understood that mastering the art of war led to enlightenment.

### Martial Arts as a Meditation

It is easily understood that the exacting style of movement training that the martial artist undergoes is an advanced form of movement meditation. The martial artist trains his body to move and react in ways never experienced by the average individual. Add to this the use of weapon, as was done with the ancient warriors of Japan, and an entirely new method of cohesive body-mind coordination is added to the meditation process.

### Zen and the Way of the Sword

Between 1595 and 1598, after years of battle, the legendary Zen Buddhist warrior, Jinsuke Shigenobu

(1546 - 1621), retreated to the Hikawa Temple to enter a period of austere meditation. During his stay he developed the meditative art of drawing the sword that he titled, *"Batto-jutsu."*

Jinsuke Shigenobu based his art upon the offensive and defensive techniques long used by the masters of the samurai sword. He integrated the understanding of *Yin and Yang* -- embrace the soft and the hard, into his newly defined system. What was born was a method where the sword practitioner, practicing alone, could focus his mind so precisely on the movement of the sword that he entered into a deep state of meditation. This art form laid the foundation for what is known in modern era as, *"Iaido."* *Iaido* is the meditative art of drawing the sword.

In the practice of *Iaido,* the practitioner acutely focuses his consciousness on the art of removing the sword from its sheath and unleashing an offensive or defensive strike. In the practice of *Iaido,* no physical opponent is ever engaged in battle. This allows the mind of the practitioner to acutely focus on the meditative aspects of this art while not being distracted by another person.

In the martial arts, any weapon that is used is understood to be an extension of the body. The sword is witnessed not as an element onto itself. Instead, it is an elongation of the arm. With this understanding, the sword becomes an integral part of the meditative process.

## Shinmyoken

The Japanese term, *"Shinmyoken"* is translated as *"Wondrous action of the soul of the sword."* This occurs when the mind is in perfect harmony with the body and the body perfectly unleashes the sword. From this focused consciousness, the experiences of drawing the sword is not witnessed as a physical activity. Instead, it is seen as simply an action that occurs in accordance with the perfection of the universe. This is the state of *action within non-action* that the Zen Buddhist strives for when practicing any form of the martial arts.

## Zen Buddhism and the Sword

The practitioner of Zen understands that each movement of life, whether it is physical or mental, must be performed with pure consciousness attached to it. From this comes a life lived in harmony.

With the conscious linking of the body and the mind, through highly advanced physical activities such as the martial arts, the individual mind is caused to focus intensely upon its actions. From this, the mind learns to possess acute focusing abilities. Therefore, from *Iaido,* or other forms of the martial arts, the Zen practitioner develops the ability to keep his mind focused upon, *"Pure thought,"* as opposed to the random roaming thoughts that are commonly guiding the mind of most individuals. With this, each action taken in association with the martial arts becomes a form of movement meditation. The practitioner of Zen may then take this understanding and apply it to all areas of his life, thereby making his every action a form of movement meditation.

# PART II
## The Metaphysical Aspects
*of Zen Buddhism*

Zen Buddhism is a spiritual pathway of paradox and contradictions. Paradox and contradictions span the entire framework of Zen Buddhism. On one hand, the techniques of Zen are very concrete -- with a primary focus upon the need for formal seated meditation. On the other hand, it is understood that each person is already enlightened and no technique will ever actually lead a person to this ultimate end. Instead, each individual must simply remember and re-embrace the fact that he is already enlightened. For these reasons, Zen Buddhism is often referred to as, *"The pathless path."*

It must be understood that the discussion of Zen is not the practice of Zen. Innumerable words have been spoken and written about the subject of Zen. These discourses are designed to define Zen Buddhism to the degree that the mind of the average individual can come to comprehend the abstract fundamentals that form the foundations of this ancient understanding.

The ironic fact of Zen Buddhism is, all Zen discourses are in exact contrast to the true essence of Zen. None-the-less, the analytical thinking mind must be provided with a set of criteria in which to guide itself towards the ultimate level of cosmic awareness. To this end, there are key ideologies that provide the Zen Buddhist practitioner with a pathway to embracing the experience of *Nirvana.*

## Chapter 5
## The Mind of No Mind

Throughout the evolution of Zen Buddhism, understandings have emerged that help to define this *pathless path*. From these detailed ideologies, the practitioner may come to more clearly understand what is expected and what may be encountered on this pathway of paradox.

### Ku

*"Ku,"* translated from Japanese means, *"Profound spiritual emptiness."* *Ku* is not an unconscious mental void. In fact, *Ku* is in complete contrast to any lack of awareness. *Ku* is a consciously encountered emptiness, achieved through acute mental focus. This conscious emptiness is the source point for the experience of *Nirvana*.

*Ku* is not a state of consciousness associated with the thinking mind. The mind of the average individual randomly travels from one thought onto the next and the next. Most people do not even choose to develop the ability to stop the thought process of their mind long enough to truly define why they are thinking what they are thinking, feeling what they are feeling, or experiencing what they are experiencing. Instead, they travel blindly through life, allowing something so temporary as a thought or an emotion to dominate their mind and the occurrences of their life experience.

Desires gives birth to thoughts. Thoughts give birth to emotions. Emotions give birth to actions. Actions give rise to *Karma*. *Karma* is the law of cause and effect -- as you sew so shall you reap. By consciously pursuing the understanding of *Ku,* Zen leads one away from the worldly path that ultimately culminates in the creation of *Karma*. Thus, the practitioner of Zen becomes free from the constraints of this worldly existence and is able to interact with the *Buddha-mind.*

*Ku* is a state of consciousness where the mind is no longer dominated by unnecessary thought patterns. In order for an individual to experience *Ku,* the foundation must be laid with the techniques designed to focus the mind. *Ku* may be achieved through the practice of *Zazen.* From *Zazen* the practitioner of Zen embraces the thoughtless mind, which is the essence of *Ku.*

**Being and Non-Being**

Zen accepts the existence of *Being*. *Being* is all that one sees, experiences, feels, and knows while the physical body binds one to this place we call life. Being is a human condition.

Zen also understands *Non-Being*. *Non-Being* can only be expressed in the state of *Ku*. *Non-Being* is present when the mind has been silenced and thoughts cease to exist.

*Non-Being* is not the thought of *no-thought*. The thought of *no-thought* is the illusion many people who meditate encounter when they train their mind to think that they are not thinking.

The practice of *Mantra* meditation, taught in many schools of yoga, replaces the random thoughts of the practitioner with a single word or phrase. Though this style of meditation focuses the mind, it does not stop the mind from thinking. It simply replaces all thoughts with one thought. Though this style of meditation may be seen as beneficial, it does not lead one to the essence of *non-being*.

*Non-Being* is at the heart of the paradox of Zen. *Non-Being* is defined by living in a human form but not being bound to the limitation of that human form. Again, this understanding details the essence of *Ku*.

## Sesshin

The Japanese word, *"Sesshin,"* means, *"The collecting of the mind."* *Sesshin* is commonly linked to the practice of *Zazen*.

Any physical or mental technique that focuses the mind can be used as a technique to achieve *Sesshin*. This is where the large difference between Zen Buddhism and the schools of Theravana Buddhism differ.

Zen embraces the necessity of all activity. No activity is more or less worthy than any other physical or mental activity. This remains true as long as the activity is performed consciously and is used as a method to focus the mind in order to encounter cosmic consciousness.

## Mushin

The Japanese word, *"Mushin"* means, *"Original Mind"* or *"No Mind."* *Mushin* witnesses a mind not bound by the desire for anything to be different than it currently is.

*Mushin* is a mindset that is not lost in judging life experiences or in judging other people. For this reason, the individual who embraces *Mushin* is like a mirror reflecting the perfection of the world.

At the heart of *Mushin* is the acceptance that things in this universe are perfect. With no desire for things to be any different than they currently are, the individual who embraces *Mushin* exists in a state of constant acceptance. From this, they are not bound by the likes and dislikes of the common individual. Thus, they are able to interact with the enlightened *Buddha-mind*.

## Ushin

*Ushin* is the opposite of *Mushin*. *Ushin* describes a mind fixated upon the temporary nature of this physical world. *Ushin* witnesses an individual believing that what he or she believes is the only right answer and that all other perceptions are incorrect. It also describes a person who is bound by desire. This is due to the fact that an individual with a mind fixated upon living and feeling a specific way is willing to do whatever it takes to maintain a specific lifestyle. From their actions, negative *Karma* is created.

The mind locked in *Ushin* is based in ego and desire. It is argumentative and confrontational. As such, this person is constantly attracting unnecessary battles, both external and internal.

*Mushin,* on the other hand, is freedom. It allows an individual to pass from moment-to-moment with no confrontation. The individual who exists in a state of *Mushin* can blend in among all people and experience the true glory of an enlightened life.

## Prajna

*Prajna* is the universal unmovable wisdom available to all people who seek its essence. *Prajna* is not unmovable in the sense of being stagnant, but unmovable in the firmness of a defined one-pointed wisdom.

*Prajna* is not a thought. *Prajna* is the instantaneousness of mastered action.

If the Zen Buddhist practitioner must contemplate his actions, then he is lost in the realms of the thinking mind and he will never understand the spontaneity that exists in the state of *Prajna*.

*Prajna* is evident when one lets go of individual ego. Individual ego is lost by coming to understand that your physical actions lead to nothing more than a movement in this transient place we call life. One's spiritual actions, on the other hand, lead to enlightenment. Therefore, by letting go of personal self and embracing the enlightened *Buddha-self,* one is allowed to leave behind the constraints of the world and experience *Nirvana*.

## Maya

*"Maya,"* is the Sanskrit word describing divine illusion. In Japanese this understanding is known as, *"Mayoi."*

The concept of *Maya* teaches us that all of life is an illusion. What we see, feel, and experience is not real. It is simply a projection of our own thinking mind.

This is where the perplexity of *Maya* is born, however. What is the thinking mind and how is it able to make us perceive a seemingly *very-real* reality if, in fact, it is all an illusion?

To the Westerner the concept of *Maya* is immediately dismissed as being an esoteric philosophy not based in empirical fact. To the practitioner of Zen Buddhism, however, this Western belief would immediately prove the existence of *Maya* -- as the Western proof that there is a standardized reality is based simply upon the consensus of unenlightened beings.

To come to understand the foundations for *Maya* it must be initially understood that everyone perceives this physical reality somewhat differently. This individual perception is based upon a person's own individual mindset that was formed by social, cultural, economic, educational, religious, and psychological events. This gives credence to the fact that there is no one absolute reality. The only reality is one that has been decided upon. Thus, physical reality is debatable.

The concept of *Maya* goes much deeper than this, however. It goes to the root of human consciousness and the basis of Zen Buddhist enlightenment.

Zen teaches us that each person is already enlightened. It is simply the veil of *Maya* that keeps us from recognizing this fact. Therefore, those who enter onto the path of Zen do so because they believe that they are separated from supreme consciousness. Thus, they begin the practices of Zen meditation hoping that at some point they may finally remove the veil of *Maya* and reach enlightenment. This, however, is understood to be the ultimate example of *Maya* -- that you must do something to reach enlightenment.

It must be understood that *Nirvana* is not based on a linear scale of higher and lower beings. Zen teaches that we all are already enlightened -- some of us simply do not choose to realize and embrace this fact.

If you choose to embrace the essence of Zen and remember your original nature, you instantaneously achieve enlightenment. Though this may seem like a perplexing paradox, this paradox is the essence of Zen. And, to break through this veil of confusion, unleashed by *Maya,* is why people refine their mind through the practice of meditation and other Zen based techniques.

The ultimate illusion of *Maya* is that there is no illusion at all. We are all enlightened -- we simply separate ourselves from this fact. Additionally, we are all locked in this physical form we call a body, which is a tool that we have been given in order to raise ourselves to clearer levels of mental, physical, and spiritual understanding.

Simply by embracing the paradoxical essence of Zen, all things fall into place and all things are understood. The veil of *Maya* is then lifted and in an instant this universe is understood and the *Buddha-mind* is encountered.

# PART III
## Nirvana

Central to the core of Buddha's teachings is that enlightenment is the ultimate end-goal for all human beings. It is believed that those who choose to walk the path towards enlightenment are on the highest pathway of human existence and, therefore, are very consciously living their life, abandoning all actions that create negative *Karma* and are moving towards the *Buddha-mind*.

It is important to keep in mind, however, that the understanding of enlightenment did not originate with the Buddha. This understanding was in existence since the dawn of advancing human consciousness.

The Pali Canons of Buddhism recorded that there were twenty-eight Buddhas or enlightened beings that existed before Siddhartha Guatama. The numbers of those who have obtained this ultimate level of human consciousness have continued to multiply throughout the centuries.

## Chapter 6
## Nirvana
### The Formalities

The Buddhist concept of *Nirvana* arose from the ancient Hindu understanding of *Samadhi*. *Samadhi*, literally translated from the Sanskrit, means, *"Ecstasy."* *Samadhi* is the supreme level of human existence. In the Yoga sutras of the Hindu sage Patangali, *Samadhi* defines the final step in human consciousness where the *individual-self* merges with the *divine-self* in a state of all-knowing *self-realization* and awareness.

There are three primary levels of *Samadhi* defined in the ancient scriptures. They are:

1. *Savikalpa Samadhi*
2. *Nirvikalpa Samadhi*
3. *Sahaja Samadhi*

### Savikalpa Samadhi

*Savikalpa Samadhi* is the stage of enlightenment where the individual has focused his or her attention upon an image of the divine and has emerged and has become one with this deity or energy. At this level of enlightenment, a person is still aware of his or her human form. They are, however, no longer defined by personality or worldly desires.

In Hinduism the worship of a supreme deity is a very common form of spiritual practice. It is known as, *"Bhakti Yoga."* Throughout the centuries various schools of Buddhism have also been known to practice a similar style of devotion -- worship and praying to the Buddha. The Zen Buddhist does not follow this path to spiritual realization, however. The Zen Buddhist understands that the Buddha reached the ultimate level of human consciousness. Once he had achieved this exalted state, he formalized a set of understandings and techniques that will cause those who practice them to become interactive with the same level of consciousness that he experienced. To this end, *Savikalpa Samadhi* is not a style of enlightenment that the Zen Buddhist seeks out. None-the-less, through his advanced meditative practices, a Zen Buddhist practitioner may encounter this level of enlightenment simply by remaining focused on the consciousness of the Buddha.

## Nirvikalpa Samadhi

The second level of *Samadhi* is known as *Nirvikalpa Samadhi*. This level of enlightenment witnesses the individual becoming devoid of self. In this *Samadhi* all levels of common bodily consciousness are lost and are replaced by complete and total cosmic consciousness. This level of enlightenment is achieved when the Zen Buddhist has allowed his or her thinking mind to be forgotten. This may be achieved through formal *Zazen* or another of the meditative practices embraced in Zen Buddhism. With the thinking mind forgotten, the universal *Buddha-mind* is embraced.

## Sahaja Samadhi

There is one final type of *Samadhi*. This is known as *Sahaja Samadhi*. This is instantaneous, total enlightenment. This is enlightenment that simply occurs in a moment of complete cosmic interaction.

It is understood in Zen Buddhism that there is no formal technique that can lead a person towards this level of supreme consciousness. Meditative techniques may train the mind to be prepared to recognize this level of *Samadhi* when it occurs, but this ultimate level of human consciousness can only be embraced when one completely lets go of *individual-self* and merges with *universal-self.* For this, there is no technique, only complete mental and physical surrender.

The individual who achieves this level of *Samadhi* is known in Sanskrit as a, *"Jivamukta," "The living liberated."* This is the style of *Nirvana* that the Buddha experienced and is the primary end-point that the Zen Buddhist walks towards.

## Chapter 7
## The Three Buddhas

Throughout the centuries Buddhism has defined three types of people who obtain the ultimate stage of enlightenment, they are known as, *"The Three Buddhas."* The Three Buddhas are:

1. *Samyaksam Buddha*
2. *Pratyeka Buddha*
3. *Sravaka Buddha*

### Samyaksam Buddha

*Samyaksam Buddha* is one who reaches enlightenment through a path that was not laid before. What this means is that the *Samyaksam Buddha* does not follow a specific teacher and does not follow a set pattern of techniques that are defined by another religion or school of philosophic thought. Instead, the *Samyaksam Buddha* finds their own pathway to enlightenment and then spreads their message to others. Siddhartha Guatama, the *Sakyamuni Buddha,* is known to be a *Samyaksam Buddha.*

### Pratyeka Buddha

The *Pratyeka Buddha* is a silent Buddha. The *Pratyeka Buddha* is an individual who has obtained the ultimate stage of human consciousness by his own means -- similar to a *Samyaksam Buddha,* yet he or she does not go on a path of leading others towards obtaining cosmic wisdom.

In the Mahayana tradition of Buddhism it is believed that only a very specific type of enlightened being possesses the power to pass on the knowledge that leads another practitioner towards enlightenment. In fact, in some sects of Buddhism, it is believed that only a fully enlightened being can actually cause a person to obtain enlightenment. The *Pratyeka Buddha,* however, is defined as one who has reached personal enlightenment, but is not capable of transmitting that ultimate level of cosmic wisdom.

### Sravaka Buddha

The *Sravaka Buddha* is one who has obtained *Nirvana* by hearing the *Dharma* and practicing it under the guidance of one who has obtained enlightenment. Due to the fact that the *Sravaka Buddha* has been schooled in all aspects of the mystic path to enlightenment, they are understood to possess the ability to teach others and guide them towards discovering their own enlightenment.

## Chapter 8
## Understanding Enlightenment

Central to the core of Zen Buddhism is the accepted understanding that we ALL are already enlightened -- we each simply need to remember and re-embrace this fact. It is further understood that it is the thinking mind of the individual that keeps him or her from embracing this obvious *self-realization.*

It is also part of the essential teachings of Zen Buddhism, however, that one cannot simply desire enlightenment. For if one has any desire for enlightenment; enlightenment will never be experienced. This is due to the fact that desire sets one apart from the ability to embrace this ultimate understanding. It is at this point that we encounter one of the supreme paradoxes of Zen Buddhism, *"The ultimate goal of Zen is enlightenment. Yet, if you seek enlightenment, it can never be found."*

This is where all of the techniques of Zen Buddhism find their basis -- as a means to shake the practitioner loose from his *thinking-*

*mind,* to make him embrace his *non-thinking* mind, in order to remove him from desire, so that he can lose all thought and achieve *Nirvana.* Here, Zen Buddhism presents one of its supreme paradoxes -- the technique of *no-technique.* The question arises, *"How can one obtain enlightenment if there is no technique?"*

The answer to this abstraction is at the root of Zen. Abstract, yet understandable, for those who have cleansed their mind of desire and dwell within a true space of ethereal silence. In this place, the Zen understanding of, *"No-desire within desire is understood."*

## Embracing Nirvana

Since the dawn of humanity there has been the concept of less and more. As human history as evolved, those who have raised themselves to the top of culture have been believed to be worthy of veneration. This is especially the case on the spiritual path. In fact, one who has obtained enlightenment is considered the highest and most holy. At the pinnacle of enlightened beings is that of Siddhartha Guatama, *the Sakyamuni Buddha.* The Buddha symbolizes all that is pure, above reproach, and at the top of the ultimate level of human existence.

We can look to the earliest Sanskrit and Pali writings and read about this exalted being and his teachings. But these writing are simply representations about this man who transcended material understanding and laid a path to higher consciousness that has been followed for centuries. Those who lived since his passing have documented the actual realizations of the Buddha and his experiences. From this style of historic legacy, legend has been born. And though legend is glorious and beautiful, legend is only that -- legend. What the Buddha actually experienced and taught is lost forever, as he never personally wrote any of his teachings down for posterity. His teachings were simply detailed by others.

This being understood, you can begin to reformulate your concept of *Nirvana* with a much clearer perception of how it affects you. For no longer must you base your definition of *Nirvana* solely upon its most exalted proponent.

*By letting go of what you expect, you will come to know.*

## Satori

The word, *"Satori,"* describes the state of instantaneous enlightenment. It is understood in Zen Buddhism that no matter how long one walks upon the spiritual path, enlightenment happens in an instant and flashes of this supreme consciousness can be invoked from virtually anything: a *Koan,* reading a spiritual text, watching a bird fly through the air, or the slap of a bamboo shaft from the *Roshi* when an individual has fallen asleep during *Zazen.*

The Zen Buddhist practitioner prepares himself or herself for this instantaneous enlightenment and willingly accepts it when it appears.

## Walking the Path to Enlightenment

Walking the path to enlightenment begins from an untold number of motivating factors. Once on this path, however, a spiritual teacher, several teachers, or simply philosophic belief may guide you. As you progress along the mystical road of Zen, you will come to realize that all of the formalities you initially held onto: your religion, your teacher, your practices, and even your own image of self begin to fall away. What remains is a pure being that is no longer bound by the traditional desires and rationales of this material world.

## Nirvana Now

Throughout history the pathway to enlightenment has been confounded by definitions and dogma set forth from an untold number of sources. This ideally illustrates the paradoxical essence of Zen that causes the practitioner to move beyond the known, the accepted, and the understood -- ultimately entering into a state of *All-Knowingness*. But, if teachings and dogma will not get you there, how does one travel the path to *Nirvana?*

*Nirvana* is the end result of the practice of Zen. The paradoxical problem that exists in this mentality is that as long as you set your sights on a goal, be it a new house, a new car, a new job, a new lover, or enlightenment, you are bound to the constraints of material existence by that desire. And, desire itself, no matter how seemingly holy, keeps you from *self-realization* and *cosmic consciousness*. Therefore, the practitioner of Zen seeks nothing but what comes naturally from each step. From this, the controlling hands of desire will not restrain you. Thus, you will be free and wholly on your pathway to enlightenment.

*Nirvana* has been defined as the ultimate step of human consciousness and evolution. For centuries, religions and spiritual teachers have defined the steps one must progress through to reach this final level of human understanding. The problem is, those who have defined the steps to enlightenment are, for the most part, self-admittedly unenlightened. How does an individual who is not enlightened, teach you how to become enlightened?

Many teachers on the Zen Buddhist pathway continually separate themselves from enlightenment by stating, *"An enlightened teacher would say..."* But, by believing that somebody else, *"Knows,"* and they do not, they continually block the possibility of encountering this most natural state of human existence. They obviously do not understand the most essential teaching of Zen, *"That we all are enlightened."*

Enlightenment is not a rank that is earned. Monkhood is a rank. Priesthood is a rank. But, enlightenment is not a rank.

In each of us, enlightenment already exists. The majority of us have simply forgotten this very obvious truth. Zen reminds us of what we have forgotten.

The plight of many practitioners and teachers alike is that they falsely believe that enlightenment is something off in the distance and not obtainable. That one must practice several lifetimes of austerities to ever touch its realms.

This common misnomer is the exact ideology that keeps so many people from encountering *Nirvana* -- their belief that it is, *"A Thing,"* that exists somewhere off in the distance. This is incorrect. Zen teaches us that enlightenment is *right here, right now*. By letting go of the known, you immediately encounter it.

Why then, do so many people live in caves for years, sit in *Zazen* for hour-after-hour, and perform forms of austerities to encounter *Nirvana?* This is the ultimate illusion of Zen, that you must do something to obtain *Nirvana*.

*Nirvana* is not about doing. *Nirvana* is about undoing. As long as you hold yourself to the belief that you are not worthy of obtaining enlightenment; that you must perform some task, overcome some *karmic* obstacle, to obtain *Nirvana, Nirvana* can never be known. So many teachers who have devoted their lives to the process of enlightenment have proven this. They have taught what they have learned from others. They have quoted the scriptures. They have lived a good life and have helped others. What they have not done, however, is to let go of the illusion that they are not enlightened.

Let go of the thoughts that you are not pure enough, not holy enough, or of a high enough incarnation to embrace *Nirvana* and it will come rushing towards you. The ultimate Zen Buddhist teaching is that, *"The only thing keeping you from Nirvana is you."* Move forward and embrace your own *Nirvana*.

## About the Author

Scott Shaw is a prolific author and filmmaker. He is recognized as one of the preeminent Martial Arts Masters of the Western World, is a leading proponent of modern Zen, and is at the forefront of integrating spirituality into the Martial Arts. During his youth he became deeply involved with Eastern Meditative Thought. This guided him to Asia where he has been initiated into Buddhist, Hindu, and Sufi sects. Today, Shaw frequently returns to Asia, documenting obscure aspects of Asian culture in words and on film. He is a frequently featured contributor to Martial and Meditative Art Journals and is the author of numerous books on Zen Buddhism, the Martial Arts, Ki Science, Yoga, and Meditation.

# Scott Shaw's
## *Books-In-Print* include:

*The Little Book of Yoga Breathing,*
*Nirvana in a Nutshell,*
*About Peace: 108 Ways to Be At Peace*
　　*When Things Are Out of Control,*
*Zen O'clock: Time To Be,*
*The Tao of Self Defense,*
*Samurai Zen,*
*The Ki Process: Korean Secrets*
　　*for Cultivating Dynamic Energy,*
*The Warrior is Silent:*
　　*Martial Arts and the Spiritual Path,*
*Hapkido: Korean Art of Self Defense,*
*Taekwondo Basics,*
*Advanced Taekwondo,*
*Chi Kung For Beginners,*
*Cambodian Refugees in Long Beach,*
　　*California: The Definitive Study,*
*Essence: The Zen of Everything,*
*Hapkido: Essays on Self-Defense,*
*Zen Buddhism: The Pathway to Nirvana,*
*Zen: Tales from the Journey,*
*Zen in the Blink of an Eye,*
*Yoga: A Spiritual Guidebook,*
*Marguerite Duras and Charles*
　　*Bukowski: The Yin and Yang of*
　　*Modern Erotic Literature.*

www.ingramcontent.com/pod-product-compliance
Lightning Source LLC
Chambersburg PA
CBHW070655050426
42451CB00008B/358